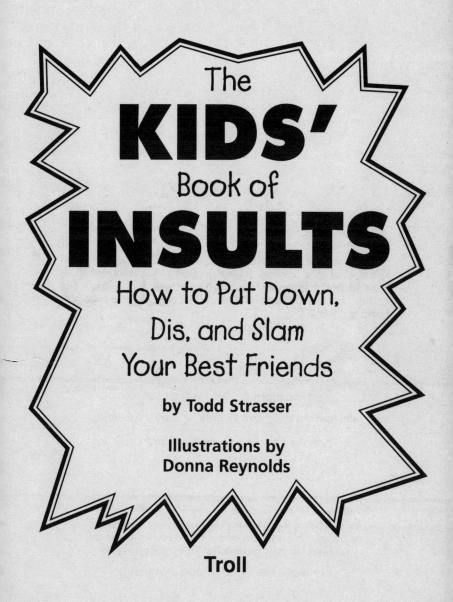

The
KIDS'
Book of
INSULTS
How to Put Down,
Dis, and Slam
Your Best Friends

by Todd Strasser

Illustrations by
Donna Reynolds

Troll

ACKNOWLEDGMENTS

No man is an island. But many islands are men.
There are women islands too. And also children
islands ... wait a minute, I got off the track.
What I meant to say was that I could not have
written this book alone. I needed a lot of help.
Without the invaluable support of the
following people this book might never have
been written. (Well ... it probably would have
been written, but it wouldn't have been as
much fun.) My sincerest thanks to:

- My wife
- My kids
- My kids' wives
- My kids' soccer coaches (Mike Plansky,
    Bob Boylan, Paul Pappas, Nate Kravis)
- My dog, Mac
- My friend
- My neighbors (with the exception of
    Mrs. Finkelsnogger)
- Anthony and Craig at Villa Maria Pizza
- Don and the guys at Hennessey Frieda
- Charles Librett Hardware
- The people who invented
    WordPerfect software
- The Grateful Dead

Additional inspiration was supplied by:

-Numerous sixth graders at The Chatsworth
   School (in particular, Kathleen Mulcahy,
   Brian Parsons, Jafar Sabet, Aaron
   Bernstein, and Justin Merolla)
-Those Gale kids
-Peter and Brett Sherman
-Various patrons of Villa Maria Pizza
-Ben and Andrew Meeker
-Pam Older
-Lia and Geoff Strasser
-Numerous third and fourth graders at the
   Windward School, including
   Jesse Goldman and Joey Paolerico
-All the trick or treaters who traded disses
   for Hershey™ Kisses
-Mrs. Ravas' seventh graders at
   Harborside Middle School
-Mrs. Foster's 8th period sixth graders from
   Atascotia Middle School
-The students of Evergreen Junior
   High School
-The students of North Middle School
   (Aurora, CO)
-Joanna Lewis Cole
-Mom

The

KIDS'

Book of

INSULTS

SCHOOL

Your armpits smell so bad your teacher gave you an A for not raising your hand.

Your butt's so big, when you go to class you sit next to everyone.

Your dandruff is so bad the principal had to declare a snow day.

You're so dumb you flunked recess.

Your armpits are so hairy, when you raise your hand the class can't see the chalkboard.

You're so thin the librarian asked you to volunteer as a bookmark.

You're so dumb you're in a class by yourself.

You're so dumb, when your teacher said she wanted you to get ahead, she really meant "a head."

HOME

Your family is so poor a rat tripped you and a cockroach stole your wallet.

Your house is so cheap, when you ring the doorbell the toilet flushes.

Your grandmother's such a bad chef even the maggots won't touch her cooking.

Your family's so poor, when you stepped on a cigarette your mom asked, "Who turned off the heat?"

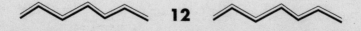

Your house is so small the front door mat only says WEL.

Your house is so small the front and back doors are on the same hinge.

Your family is so poor, when you asked what was for dinner your mother held up her feet and said "corns."

Your family is so poor, when someone rings the doorbell your mom sticks her head out the window and goes, "Ding! Dong!"

Your family's so poor the family vehicle is a skateboard.

DUMB AND DUMBER

Your brother's so dumb he thought Jungle Gym was Tarzan's brother.

Your father's so dumb he had to go to college just to work his way up to stupid.

Your sister's so dumb she dreamed about a muffler and woke up exhausted.

Your little brother's so dumb he thought Christmas Eve was Santa Claus' wife.

Your mother's so dumb the mind reader gave her 50% off his bill.

Your aunt's so dumb, when I said it was chilly outside, she got a bowl.

Your big brother's so dumb he's studying to be a crash dummy.

Your big sister's so dumb she went to the drive-in movie theater to see "Closed for the Season."

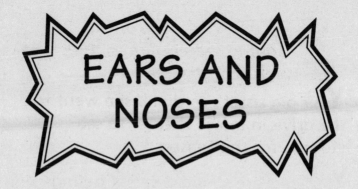

EARS AND NOSES

Your nostrils are so hairy they're a car wash for your micro machines.

Your nose hairs are so long you have a built-in toothbrush.

Your nose is so ugly the only thing worse is what's inside.

Your nose hairs are so thick your sinuses need flashlights.

Your ears are so big a basset hound asked you for a date.

Your ears are so big your parents wanted to use you as a satellite dish.

Your nostrils are so hairy people think you have a moustache.

Your nose is so big the only dates you get are with anteaters.

RELATIVES

Your father's so slow he can't even catch his breath.

Your nephew's so dumb he put his watch in the bank to save time.

Your grandmother's so feeble the only thing she does fast is fall asleep.

Your dog's so dumb he couldn't find a bone in a butcher shop.

Your cousin's so stupid, when the movie said, "No one under 17 allowed," he went home and got 16 of his friends.

Your brother's so lazy they thought he was in a coma.

Your aunt is so fat she's on both sides of the family.

Your grandfather is so bald dragonflies use his head as a runway.

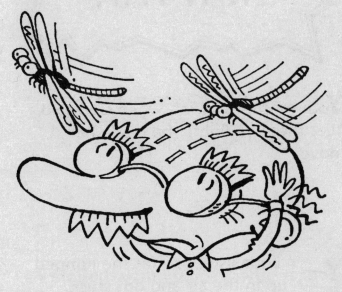

Your dog is so slow he brings in last week's paper.

Your aunt's so fat she asked for a waterbed and they threw a blanket over the Atlantic Ocean.

HOW FAT?

Your mother's so fat, when God said, "Let there be light," he made her move.

Your sister's so fat she jumped up in the air and got stuck.

Your brother's so fat, when he goes backwards you hear "Beep, beep, beep!"

Your mother's so fat she irons her clothes in the driveway.

Your sister's so fat, when she wears a yellow dress, people yell, "Taxi!"

Your baby brother's so fat he has to use a fork lift for a high chair.

Your dad's so fat he wears two watches — one for each time zone.

You're so fat you have your own zip code.

You're so fat you had to be baptized at Water World.

Your mother's so fat, when she sits around the house, she *really* sits *around* it!

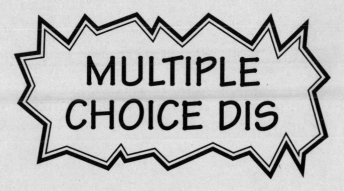

MULTIPLE CHOICE DIS

Your father's so stupid:

a) He took half an hour to make Minute Rice.

b) He thought he was a great artist because everyone gave him "the brush off."

c) He thought a quarterback was a refund.

d) He tripped over the cord on a cellular phone.

e) When his friend invited him to play pool, he brought a bathing suit.

Your sister's so ugly:

a) She has ears that make Dumbo jealous.

b) Her pillow cries at night.

c) The doctor wanted to do a head transplant.

d) When she was born the doctor slapped your mother.

e) When she went to the beach the tide refused to come in.

FEET

Your feet are so big you'd be disqualified from a swim meet for wearing flippers.

Your feet are so smelly your shoes hid in the closet and refused to come out!

Your feet are so big a cop pulled you off the sidewalk and asked for your license and registration.

Your feet are so big, when you dance you step on everyone's toes.

Your feet are so big you don't need water skis.

Your toenails are so long you cut the grass by walking barefoot.

Your feet smell so bad you have to keep your shoes on to fight pollution.

FAT AND FATTER

Your father's so fat he uses a VCR as a beeper.

Your mother's so fat they parasail with her underwear.

Your mother's so fat, when she goes to the beach she's the only one who gets tan.

Your aunt is so fat, when she wore an orange dress bungee jumping, people thought the sun was falling.

Your uncle's so fat he went to Weight Watchers and they shut the gate.

Your brother's so fat the sign on his car says "Wide Load."

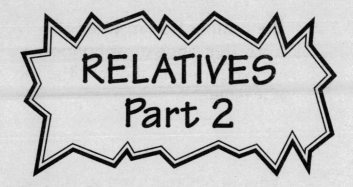

RELATIVES
Part 2

Your cousin is so wide, when she was missing they put her picture on a milk truck.

Your niece is so fat her Levi's don't say 501, they say 747.

Your aunt's lips are so big she puts lipstick on with a spray gun.

Your little brother is so stupid he locked himself in the bathroom and wet his pants.

Your aunt's teeth are so yellow all she has to do to see in the dark is smile.

Your grandmother's armpits are so hairy it looks like she's got Cher in a headlock.

Your uncle's such a dork he must be smarter than he looks.

Your cousins's so slow he ran a bath and came in last.

Your dog's so dumb he chases parked cars.

WHAT'S EATING YOU

Your uncle's so dumb he thought an Italian hero was someone who got a medal.

Your father's so thick he got fired from the M&M factory for throwing out the Ws.

Your brother eats so much he uses a shovel and pitchfork for silverware.

Your father's so thick he thought Taco Bell was a phone company.

Your sister is so fat, when she sat on a rainbow, Skittles fell out.

Your uncle's so poor he licks the customers' fingers at KFC.

You're so small you use a Dorito for a hang glider.

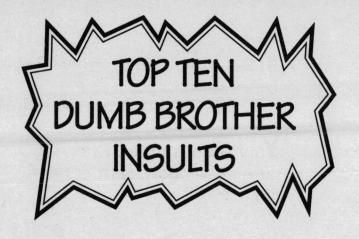

TOP TEN DUMB BROTHER INSULTS

Your brother's so dumb:

1) He jumped off a building and had to stop and ask for directions.

2) They examined his head and couldn't find anything.

3) He left his brain to science, but they wouldn't accept it.

4) He stared at the orange juice container because it said "concentrate."

5) He drew a line for the 50-yard dash.

6) He started a campaign to save the polyester.

7) He lost his mind and didn't notice.

8) He got athlete's foot so he could run faster.

9) He stuck his head in the microwave to get a hot idea.

10) He went to buy a TV but couldn't decide on the color.

Bonus: When his teacher said he had to brush up on spelling, he bought a tooth brush.

ODORS

Your breath is so bad your orthodontist tried to wire your mouth shut.

Your mother's breath is so bad the government wants to use her as a secret weapon.

Your father's breath is so bad, when he jogs through the park the bark falls off the trees.

Your dad smells so bad, when he put on Right Guard, it left.

Your brother's breath is so bad his dentist had to give himself gas.

Your breath is so bad even the telephone operator has to hold her nose.

Your dog's breath is so bad even skunks run away.

Your sister's breath is so bad she has to gargle with antifreeze.

Your brother's breath is so bad he must have swallowed his gym socks.

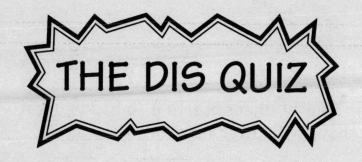

MATCH COLUMN A TO COLUMN B:

Your legs are so thin ...

Your watch is so cheap ...

Your dog's so ugly ...

Your nose is so big ...

Your pimples are so big ...

You're so dumb you thought ...

The grass wilts before he goes.

They show up on radar.

It only goes up to 9 o'clock.

The First Lady was a pilgrim.

They nicknamed you Chopsticks.

Your friends can slalom on it.

SKINNY

Your aunt's so skinny she swallowed a marble and everyone thought she was pregnant.

You're so skinny you look like a ski pole with hair.

Your brother's so skinny he does push-ups under the door.

HOW UGLY?

Your brother's so ugly, when he was born they put tinted windows on the incubator.

Your sister's hairstyle is so ugly the cat coughed up a nicer one.

You're so ugly they made you the goalie so you'd have to wear a mask.

Your brother's so ugly he threw a boomerang and it wouldn't come back.

Your clothes are so ugly even the scarecrow wouldn't wear them.

Your mother's so ugly her tears run down the back of her head so they won't have to see her face.

Your girlfriend's so ugly even the garbage collectors won't pick her up.

Your little brother's so ugly he played hide-and-seek and no one looked for him.

You're so ugly they call you "The Exterminator" because you kill bugs on sight.

Your mother's so ugly she fell into the Amazon River and scared the piranhas.

DISCELLANEOUS

Your cousin's neck is so red, when he walks down the street, cars stop.

Your brother's so filthy he lost five pounds taking a bath.

Your mom's teeth are so yellow I can't believe it's not butter.

Your sister smells so bad even the flies wear gas masks.

You're in such bad shape you get exhausted just riding the escalator.

Your mom's cooking is so bad you went to Roto-Rooter for dinner.

Your belly button has so much lint your grandmother knitted a sweater.

Your cousin's so tall, when they say his head's in the clouds, they're not kidding.

Your sister's acne is so bad her tears need a 4X4 to get down her face.

HOW THICK?

Your brother's so thick he sat on the TV and watched the couch.

You're so thick, when the soccer coach said you were a sweeper, you brought a broom.

Your cousin's so thick it takes him two hours to watch *60 Minutes*.

Your brother's so thick, when your mom said, "Make your bed," he went to the lumber yard.

Your sister's so thick she got hit by a parked car.

Your uncle's so thick he got stabbed in a gun fight.

Your mom's so thick she sent you to rehab because you were hooked on phonics.

TOP TEN UGLY BOYFRIEND/ GIRLFRIEND INSULTS

Your boyfriend/girlfriend is so ugly:

1) I'd rather kiss a head of lettuce.

2) When he went to the zoo, the monkeys laughed.

3) The shower drain has nicer hair.

4) He had to put a pork chop around his neck to get his dog to follow him.

5) She went to the dog show and won first place.

6) His mother got a ticket for littering when he was born.

7) She used to look for dates on the Most Wanted list.

8) His parents rented out his baby videos as horror films.

9) When she was born her parents didn't know which end to diaper.

10) He couldn't take out the garbage.

THE REST OF YOU

Your burps are so loud they register on the Richter scale.

Your braces are so big you set off the metal detector at the airport.

Your arms are so hairy the mosquitos need a lawn mower.

Your zits are so bad they served your face as a pizza pie.

Your ears are so waxy your mom stuck wicks in them and used your head for a candle.

Your legs are so hairy you wear pigtails for an ankle bracelet.

Your neck is so dirty your mother thought you were wearing a turtleneck.

You're so hairy you're an insult to Big Foot.

Your fingernails are so dirty a tree grew under your thumb.

You're so ugly your mother uses a slingshot to feed you.

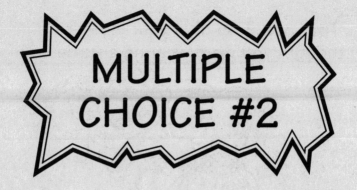

MULTIPLE CHOICE #2

You're so skinny:

a) You use a Cheerio for a hula hoop.

b) Your shadow had to find a new job.

c) You use a Band-Aid for a bathing suit.

You're so clumsy:

a) You slept on the floor and still fell out of bed.

b) When you fell off a bench, you fell off all sides.

c) You ran into a parked car and yelled, "Hey, watch where you're going!"

DISCELLANEOUS 2

You're so weak you couldn't beat an egg.

Your hair's so greasy they asked
you to be a supplier for Jiffy Lube.

Your girlfriend's clothes are so ugly, the only thing uglier is the person wearing them.

Your cousin's such a geek he wears galoshes in the shower.

Your grandmother's so boring she won't even talk to herself.

Your mother talks so much she wears a sign that says, "Open 24 Hours."

Your brother's so slow he raced a pregnant lady and came in third.

Your sister's teeth are so big she made a beaver jealous.

Your sister's been in the same grade so long people think she's the teacher.

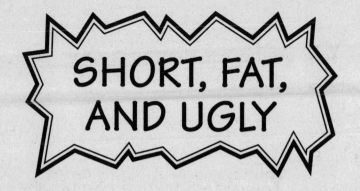

SHORT, FAT, AND UGLY

You're so short, when you sit on the curb your feet dangle.

Your mom's so fat she sees *90210* every time she steps on the bathroom scale.

Your sister's so ugly, when she looked in the mirror her reflection barfed.

You're so short, when you grow up you'll still be short.

You're so ugly the only dates you get are on a calendar.

You're so fat your first word was "oink."

HOW STUPID CAN YOU GET?

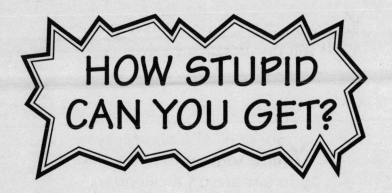

You're so stupid, the day you graduated from kindergarten you cut yourself shaving.

Your sister's so stupid she thought YMCA was Macy's spelled wrong.

You're so stupid you went into an antique shop and asked, "What's new?"

Your brother's so stupid he sold his car for gas money.

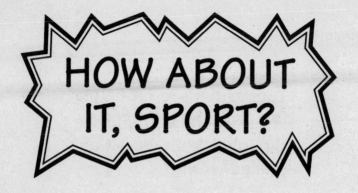

HOW ABOUT IT, SPORT?

Your brother's so fat, when they ask him to play touch football, he's the field.

Your father's so fat he plays pool with the planets.

Your brother's so dumb he thought a hat trick involved doves.

Your aim is so bad you threw a rock at the ground and missed!

Your brother's so stupid he paid for a free throw!

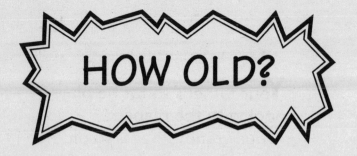

HOW OLD?

Your grandmother's so old they gave her a birthday and called the fire department to put out the cake.

Your grandfather is so old he remembers when the Dead Sea was just sick.

Your great aunt's so old she drinks formaldehyde to stay preserved.

Your grandmother is so old her birthdate expired.

Your great aunt's so old she was a waitress at the Last Supper.

Your great uncle's so old, when they say he "looks like a million," they're serious.

Your grandfather's so old he went to an antiques auction and people bid on *him.*

Your great uncle's so old even his teeth have wrinkles.

Your grandmother's so old, when she went to school, history was current events.

TOP TEN FAT SISTER INSULTS

Your sister is so fat:

1) She saw a bus going down the street and yelled, "Stop that Twinkie!"

2) When she was born your mother wanted to name her Montana.

3) She got hit by a car and asked, "Who threw that rock?"

4) Her blood type is "Ragu."

5) The only reason there's day and night is because she walks back and forth.

6) She hula hoops with the rings of Saturn.

7) They asked her to check her bags when she wasn't carrying any!

8) She has to take a bath in the Pacific Ocean.

9) They ran a marathon around her.

10) When she wears high heels she strikes oil.

Bonus: **She cut her leg and bled gravy.**

LAST RESORT

You're so stupid...

you're an insult to stupid people.

SPECIAL NOTE ON THE USE OF INSULTS

Insults are cruel. There is already enough meanness and nastiness in the world, and books filled with insults will only make it worse. Therefore the author (whoever he really is) asks that you enjoy this book for its humor value only.

Please don't use fat insults on overweight people or stupid insults on people who, for whatever reason, aren't as smart as you. Being mean or cruel will not impress your friends. It may scare them into *pretending* to like you. But deep down they'll think you're a jerk.

However, if you really feel the need to insult someone, the following is a list of people you should try to insult as often as possible:

1) Dictators of Third World countries who routinely violate human rights laws.

2) Drug dealers, and people who sell cigarettes or liquor to minors.

3) People who litter and/or pollute the environment.

4) Drivers who tailgate.*

*If you read this book and are old enough to drive, the author suggests you get help fast.

About the Author

Todd Strasser is not the author's real name. The person who actually wrote this book invented and patented the dis (slam, rank out, put down, etc.). He makes money every time someone disses someone else. This has made him the richest man in the world. He is so rich that he is presently the king of South America. King Todd owns many multinational corporations, several gold mines, Australia, and the NFL. He thinks up new disses while relaxing in his castle beside his private ocean. He is a compulsive liar.

About the Author (Seriously)

Todd Strasser has written many award-winning novels for young and teenage readers. Among his best-known books are *Help! I'm Trapped in Obedience School* and *How I Changed My Life*. He and his wife and children were last seen on video holding up a bank to get enough money to cover a check that bounced.

HEY! WANNA GET YOUR NAME IN A BOOK?

Writing books of insults is hard work. If you would like to make the job easier, and maybe even get to see your name in a book, send your insults and disses to:

TODD STRASSER
C/O TROLL COMMUNICATIONS
100 CORPORATE DRIVE
MAHWAH, NJ 07430-1404